Prayers for Animals

D0094422

Prayers
for
Animals

Carol J. Adams

continuum
NEW YORK • LONDON

2004

The Continuum International Publishing Group Inc
15 East 26 Street, New York, New York 10010

The Continuum International Publishing Group Inc
The Tower Building, 11 York Road, London SE1 7NX

Printed in the United States of America

Library of Congress Cataloging-in-Publication Data

Adams, Carol J.
Prayers for animals / Carol J. Adams.
p.   cm.
Includes bibliographical references.
ISBN 0-8264-1651-9 (pbk. : alk. paper)
1. Prayers for animals.   2. Animal welfare—religious aspects.
I. Title.
BV283.A63A33   2004
242'.8—dc22   2004005713

Continuum Publishing is committed to preserving ancient forests
and natural resources. We have elected to print this title on 30%
postconsumer waste recycled paper. As a result, this book has saved:
3.6 trees
1050 gallons of water
615 kw hours of electricity
9 lbs of air pollution
Continuum is a member of Green Press Initiative, a nonprofit pro-
gram dedicated to supporting publishers in their efforts to reduce
their use of fiber obtained from endangered forests. For more infor-
mation, go to www.greenpressinitiative.org.

for
Bruce,
twenty-five years
of answered prayers

Content

When something troubles me, I have two choices: I can take it to God in prayer or take it to God by encountering God through the created world. In particular, I can take what troubles me to God or to the ducks.

As Evelyn Underhill observes, prayer, like the whole of our inner lives, swings between the unseen and the seen.

When I take my troubles to the ducks, I take them to several kinds of ducks who live year round at Cottonwood Park. There they are busy with their lives. The early morning finds them enjoying a sprinkler bath, before the birdseed man arrives to call them to the basketball court where they gather to enjoy their breakfast. In the late afternoon, standing on one leg, with their heads tucked into their wings, they rest. Not only ducks gather there, but geese, egrets, herons, cormorants, pigeons, squirrels, turtles, ants, bees, flies, fishes, *waterbugs, dogs and their companions. Experts tell us there are between 30 million and 100 million living species on the Earth; the creatures who populate Cottonwood Park hint at this immense variety.*

The "seen" world announces that we share life on this Earth with an amazing diversity of beings.

When I take my troubles to God, I take them to the Friend, the Comforter, the One who Heals.

There are probably millions of names for the Unseen, all of them, to an extent, inadequate, yet each name acknowledges an eternal truth: God is the One who listens to our prayers.

Prayer is an active engagement with that which is beyond our understanding, beyond our comprehension, yet something continually present to us.

Praying connects us directly to the sources of our suffering and the Source of our healing.

Everyone who loves an animal can grow through praying.

Everyone who prays can be awakened to love for all creatures.

Prayer, itself a creative act, links us to the Creator and to Creation. Through prayer, we are one with all of God's creatures.

Prayer is where love of God and love of animals, the unseen and the seen, meet together.

Each of us can be helped by prayer, and animals can be helped, too.

People often feel deep emotions in response to the lives of animals. Learning of one animal's suffering or many animals' suffering may touch us very deeply. Sometimes we do not want to be that deeply touched because we know how much it hurts to care about another's suffering. Praying for animals allows us to unburden ourselves of these feelings by sharing them. In opening ourselves, we are kept open to the lives of others.

People who care about other animals' suffering often feel powerless; prayer transforms powerlessness.

Prayers of adoration and petition as well as prayers of activism all touch the Created Order, connecting us to the Oneness of Creation.

The world overwhelms us; we retreat and pray for ourselves and the world, and right relationships.

The world delights us; we pause and acknowledge thanksgiving for our connections, for the unity of life.

We can pray with our hands and with our hearts; we can pray with our actions and with our silence.

We can pray by acknowledging our pain. Prayer speaks of our weakness to the One who is strong. Prayer asks, acknowledges, connects, releases, reveals.

This book provides a series of prayers that arc through the day. It offers prayers that respond to the kinds of outward and inward concerns about animals that each day may generate from its beginning through its activities to its close. It begins with morning prayers and prayers of adoration, and then moves to prayers that center on our relationships to creatures and the Creator.

In the middle of the book, you will find prayers that focus on our special friendships with animals who live with us. Of necessity, prayers of mourning and grief follow. Where loving relationships exist, surely, too, death will enter. In a world that responds to these deaths with the comment, "just a dog," "just a cat," "just a rabbit," the aching heart searches for words that witness to the specific loss of an animal friend. I have myself deeply grieved the death of my friends, and draw in part on my own bereavement in shaping these prayers. Importantly, the series of mourning prayers recognize that the grieving process occurs over *a period of time. One cannot hurry it, nor ignore it, nor simply replace that friend with a new one.*

Prayers of Petition and Intercession extend our focus to the household of Earth, all creatures imperiled at this time. The book closes with a few evening prayers.

I would like to note some special prayers that can be used by parents on behalf of a child's relationship with animals, prayers of both friendship and of mourning (page 52, page 74). A couple of prayers speak in a child's voice, so as to incorporate children into prayerful relations with animals (pages 22, 73, 125).

Another dimension of these prayers is that a few of them speak to what may seem to be unusual situations: for instance, a prayer for an animal whose human companion dies, or a prayer after a child has dreamt of an animal friend who recently died.

When one begins to think of the variety of our relationships with animals, a remarkable number of situations present themselves. Some of them have found their ways into prayers in this book. I would welcome comments from readers about relationships or situations that I have not addressed in this book.

Together, these prayers assure, grieve, exult, adore, thank, provoke new spiritual thoughts and connections, pray for change and comfort, and reflect on the individual's connection to and response to God, Creator, Ground of Our Being, and to animals. Like prayer itself, this book tries to concentrate attention.

Prayer does not cut God down to our size, but finds ways always to expand our own limited experiences of God.

Prayer allows us to accept our contradictions, the best we desire yet the jealousies we harbor and the selfishness that limits us. It is often in relationships with other animals that these contradictions are palpable.

Prayer is an unembarrassed space that welcomes the embarrassed self.

Prayer awakens us to the mystery and majesty of the world.

Prayer attunes us to relationship.

We can pray out of thankfulness for the way creation touches us, through the rays of the sun and the light of the moon, through the sounds of an animal near us, or the thoughts of an animal far from us.

Prayer does not solely seek transformation; prayer is an act of transformation.

Praying shapes chards into pottery.

Prayer allows inward change because it makes us open to a spirit, a spirit that becomes available to us as we pray.

Praying reminds us: We—the seen and the unseen—are One.

Morning Prayers and Prayers of Adoration

God, I know you are present in my life.
You are present in my waking and my sleeping
    and my going forth.
God, I know you are present in my life
    through the animals in my life.
You are present in their waking and their sleeping
    and their daily going forth.
God, for these animals,
    a hundredfold thanks.
God, thank you for the morning.
    In the morning both the animals and I stretch our
        bodies and greet the day.
God, thank you for sleep.
    In our sleep, the animals and I dream.
And God, thank you for my life in the world.
    When I go into it I know I am not alone.
You are with me
    And in so many ways, so are Your animals.
This is a blessing.
A daily blessing.
A blessing in my waking and sleeping
    and in my going forth.

God of safe spaces and loving places,

You know that every morning is a good morning for
    chickens.

My friends who run a sanctuary know it too:

They say, Every morning is a good morning for
    chickens

    who are free to peck and stretch and roam
    outside.

May this be true for me, too

    In the sanctuary of Your love

    May every morning be a good morning.

Thank You for the lessons to be learned from Your
    creatures.

Thank You for each and every good morning.

Do the birds sing Your praises this morning?
Listening One, I don't pretend to know.
The whippoorwill, the bobolink, the chickadee
Even their names sing out to us.
   We who named them.
But we can not know to whom their songs point.
Must they point somewhere?
I pray that I do not pretend
   that my hearing makes their song complete,
But I do know that Your hearing
   makes my prayer complete.

O Mysterious One,
Today I would like to see the world
    the way animals do.
But I cannot see around the back of me like a rabbit.
I cannot see in the night, like an owl.
I cannot tower above the trees like a giraffe.
But I can celebrate the gift of life and its diversity.
I can rejoice in long necks and strong hind legs
    and powerful eyes.
And I can be thankful.
    Thankful for the ways I am like other animals.
    And thankful for the ways animals are different
        from me
            and from one another.
Today I can see Your marvelous world.
And rejoice that I am a part of it.

Holy is Your Creation.

The butterfly going past my window,

Am I the one trapped behind glass?

Am I trapped behind more than glass

    that keeps me

    from realizing with joy

Holy is Your Creation.

God of all feathered beings,

Thank you for birds.

Thank you for their early morning songs.

I, too, lift a song to heaven when morning breaks.

This song of praise.

For redwing blackbirds.

For robins bathing outside the window.

For peacocks and cassowarys

For the ostrich and the egret

For the loon and the petrel

For the pelican and seagull.

Have You not gathered us the way a mother hen
gathers her chicks?

I pray for chickens who can't gather their chicks.

Who live in cages the size of an innocent man's
cell.

Great God, the largest space they will know is
the oven.

How can we treat Your feathered world so
cruelly?

And Great God, how can baby chicks be thrown
away?

The morning song of a bird announces a newly
dawning day, fresh, with new life.

Great God, give us fresh spirits.
Can we gather the baby chicks under our wings
     as we celebrate Your creation?
          Your feathered beings,
               The woodpecker and the heron and the pigeon
               And yes, the chicken.
God, You know my imperfections.
          I ignore the baby chick within.
All that is fresh and new, and desires growth,
     Sometimes I ignore it or fight it.
I am sometimes too fragile to allow the new within to
     survive.
Create within me the ability to greet each day like
          Your birds.
And to care for animals as You would, God,
     You who would gather us all within
          Your outstretched
          wings.

God of the new day and the newborn,

    Greet me again this day, this moment.

The birth of an animal is not always good

    yet newborns excite us.

God, give us more than excitement.

Give us a sense of responsibility.

God of the midday and the middle years,

    I shall try to greet you here, again and again.

    Here at the animal shelters.

    Here where animals are abandoned.

    We seemed to promise them more than this

        when they were born.

God of the setting sun and extinguished lives,

    Help me care for animals.

Your unknown world is so vast, God.

It reminds me that You did not create it for us only,
      the two-legged.

I marvel God that one-fifth of all known animals are
      beetles!

When I think of the ground beetles
         the tiger and long-horned beetles
         the leaf and death-watch beetles
         the ladybugs, fireflies, glowworms, and
           whirligigs,

I am not surprised that it has been said, God
     that You seem inordinately fond of beetles.

There are beetles who burrow, bore, chew, fly.

How well you armored them, God!

How creative You are!

Dear God, I recall the story of the scientist who
      counted
     all the species of beetles on one tree in Panama.
     He found that there were more unknown species
     than known.
        You know them all.

If that many species of beetles tell us anything,

It is that, for us, the unknown and the unnamed
      outnumber the known and the named.

You are vast God

Your beetles tell me this.

Dear God,

Today I lift my voice in praise and thanksgiving
for all the wonderful beings who exist in this
world.

Today I lift my voice in praise and thanksgiving,
for those wonderful beings with whom I live.

Today I lift my voice in praise and thanksgiving
for the small and the large,
those near and those far,
for the two-legged and the four-legged and the
no-legged.

And today, I remember in my heart and my prayers:
Elephants who have lost a loved one,
Chimpanzees and gibbons, and other cousins of
ours sold in captivity,
Worms washed onto sidewalks by rain who die.

I remember in my heart and my prayers:
those with names and those with no names,
the small and the large, those near and those far,
those who walk and those who are unable to
walk.

I remember in my heart and my prayers:
those who because of cages cannot this day even
lift their wings
or move their bodies.

Today I lift my voice in praise and thanksgiving,
And I remember all of us
    Your animals
        in my heart
            and in my prayers.
And I know that today I have work to do.

To the mole, You are the Ground.

To the eagle, the Sky.

To the bluejay babies,

      You are a Nest of twigs and string.

To the dog at the shelter,

      You are a Ride to a new home.

You—below, above,

    enclosing, freeing.

You—foundation and new life,

    presence and promise.

May I know You as they know You.

May I help You be known.

For Our Relationships with Creatures and the Creator

Creator, I begin here.

Because I worship You, I worship the animals in You,

I worship You in the animals.

Because I worship You Creator

I want to worship the anteaters, armadillos, aardvarks,
angwantibos.

Yes, and then I will worship the bats, bandicoots,
baboons
the beavers, bears, badgers, bobcats, boars,
bongo, buffalo, bison,
And the cats, capuchins, chimpanzees, civets,
coyotes, cheetahs.

I'm only beginning Great One.
There are camels, caribou, cavies, capybara, and
chinchilla, too.

I worship the dogs, ducks, dingoes, dolphins, deer,
dik-diks, dormouse
the elephants, ermines, elands,
and the foxes and ferrets as well.

O most Holy One, there are gibbons, gorillas,
gophers,
giraffes, gerbils, gazelles, and goats to worship,

And horses, hyenas, hedgehogs, hyraxes, hogs,
hippopotami, and

Indri, impala, ibex

Jaquars and jerboas

Kangaroos and koalas

Lemurs, loris, languars, leopards, lemmings, lynx,
      lions,

      Mice, moles, moonrats, manatees, marmosets,
      monkeys, moose

      Mongoose, muskrats, macaques, mandrills,
      mangabeys, minks.

O God, I worship the narwhals, the nyala, nilgai,
      nutria

      The oppossum, orangutans, otters, ocelots,
      okapi, oryx, orcas, and ox.

I worship the pigeons, platypus, possums, pangolins,
      pandas, polecats, and

      The porcupine, pika, porpoises, pigs, and
      peccaries.

I worship the rhinoceri, rats and raccoons, rheboks
      and rabbits

      The sloths, the sheep, shrews, skunks, sea lions,
      seals, sassabys.

I worship the Tasmanian devils, tarmarin, tigers,
      tapirs, tuco-tucos

And the whales, wolves, wombats, woodchucks,
　　wallabys, weasels, wildebeests
The walrus, warthogs, wapiti, and waterbucks.
Even as I worship the yaks, zebras and zokor
　　I am only beginning.
God I want to worship
　　the birds, the fish, the reptiles, too.
I do not know their own names for themselves.
But if I see You in all beings and all beings in You
　　do names matter?

Great One, I begin here.
　　Worshiping You in the animals,
　　I worship the animals in You.

Seamstress God,

    You who thread all beings together

Breadmaker God,

    You who shape us

Child-tenderer God,

    You who care for the young and vulnerable

Stitch me, shape me, touch me, hear me—

    Make me one with all You have created.

Your world is impermanent, God.

I cannot see a tree grow, yet I know it does.

    Your seasons teach me that.

Your world is impermanent, God.

    That is why I love it so.

Dear God,

I read of a man who for 50 dollars bought a plot of
      land in New York City because
           it held a 300-year-old oak tree.

During the holidays, he gathered shelled walnuts and
      cracked watermelon
           and sunflower seeds.

Then he hiked to his lot with his seed treats
           and hung them from the tree.

He did not want those who wintered there to be
      forgotten.

He said, DO NOT THINK OF ME AS SANTA CLAUS.

      RATHER, REGARD ME AS A RELATIVE OF A

      HOUSEHOLD OF SQUIRRELS AND BIRDS.

God, thank You for this man.

Thank You for each person who, like him, cares for
      their relatives.

Plant within each of us a spirit of gift-giving.

Help us see the Earth as our Household,

      And the squirrels and birds and all creatures as
      our relatives.

God, I feel captive to my own responsibilities.
I move through each day, burdened,
    heavy with demands.
I have lost sight of You.
God, grant that I, like the woodcock,
    who with that chunky and short body
    seems born to be Earthbound
God, grant that I, like the woodcock,
    could rise above the gravity of my life.
Grant me a flight
        of barrel rolls
          and arches
        loop the loops
          and twists

So that I can see You again in the tasks
    that await me.

O Holy One,

Sometimes I feel I understand animals better than I
understand You.

The beavers build their homes in water.

If there has been damage, they repair it.

You, according to the great story of the Flood and
Noah,

when You felt there had been damage to Your
creation,

destroyed almost all human and nonhuman
animals.

I know of no animal who has been *that* destructive.

Now, the world of humans seems so destructive.

Could it be we all, God and human, have lessons to
learn from the beaver?

Help me learn from the beavers how to repair my
home, the world.

You do not waste Your time looking at us.

When You smell our scent, You are rightly suspicious.

You do not gossip, embarrass, revile.

You do not kill for entertainment or to hang
        something on Your wall.

When we are noisy, You are silent.

You are right to avoid us.

Contact with us brings death or captivity.

To You, we may seem irrelevant.

As You look away, run away, avoid us, You say

    I am not yours, though you will try to make it so.

God, I think I know about abandonment.

I have cared for abandoned animals.

    To know of their abandonment tears at my heart.

I have discovered dogs on walks, without collars,

    Without companions, without safety.

I have worried for all abandoned animals—

    the dogs dropped off,

    the downed cows at the door of slaughterhouses,

    the bunnies, cats, ducks left off in towns and

        cities,

    Ponds and human-built creeks, populated with

        beings that

        people tired of.

Are commitments to another being that hard to keep?

I should know.

I, too, have felt abandoned, have felt so small, so

    fragile.

But God, You are the One who really knows

    abandonment.

We abandon You.

Emerge God,

    Emerge from my own abandonment.

Are Your angels really hovering in the sky?

Because I think I just saw one walking by

    Leaving paw prints in the snow

    Cloven tracks in the mud

    A slug trail on the sidewalk

    Hoofprints . . . .

How near they are.

How holy they are.

God of stillness,

I am rushed—

    It is hard to take a moment and think of You.

        Harder even, to think of Your Creation.

When I am rushed

    My thoughts can be on me.

    What I have to do.

When I am rushed

    I believe in my self-importance.

    People need me!

    Tasks require me!

When I am rushed

    I don't have to listen.

    I don't have to change.

I need a park bench in my mind

    Where I can sit for a moment

    Where I can slow my mind down, God.

And in this park bench in my mind,

    As I sit there, a few birds face me,

    And a squirrel, sitting still, studies a nut,

I think I'll take this park bench where

    I can see deer, too.

    And in the afternoon, monarch butterflies.

    And at sunset, the red fox.

They each have their own pace, their own rhythm.

    What rhythm is mine?

When I am rushed, sit me down

    on that park bench, Living God

And let me find a rhythm in pace with Your Creation.

God of stillness, in my haste,

    help me remember that I am part of

      Your Creation

        And that we are all Yours.

God of all growing things,
Thank you for peppers.
    Seeding them,
      I am reminded of a cycle of growth
          And my part in it.
      We all begin somewhere.
          I am here, God.
Here with chili peppers, zucchini, eggplants,
      tomatoes—
    the fruits of Your garden.
God of all gardens,
Thank you for vegetables and fruits.
    Picking them, washing them, preparing them,
    I am reminded of a cycle of growth.
    We all grow toward something.
    Plants grow toward the sun,
      I grow toward You.
God of the sun,
Thank you for that energy that the plants absorb as
      their food.
    And for plants that nourish me.
God of all beings, like a mustard seed
    my thoughts have grown.
Keep their roots in Your soil.
    May their fruits be of Your spirit.

Ground of our Being

You from whom we find our strength

You upon whom we stand

Thank You for the Earth

Thank You for the earthworm.

Dear God,

Today I saw the most wonderful thing:

    ducks walking on ice—

        carefully.

There was an aching beauty to it all—

    The frozen trees in the sunlight.

    The ice on the tree limbs glistening and reflecting

      the sun's rays.

Yet, the sun was melting this beauty.

    Beads of water hanging from limbs and branches

    Made teardrops in the tree.

    There was a frozen majesty to the park.

Most of the ducks and the geese were in just one

      unfrozen area of the large pond

        swimming around.

    Except for the ducks walking on ice—

      carefully.

When the ducks landed on the ice

    Were they surprised by this unsteady and

      slippery place they landed on?

God, I also know unsteady and slippery places.

    Sometimes, I am the unsteady and slippery place.

    I am not the solid ground.

    I am not on solid ground.

I am thrown off when I try to land.

I want to do so much, I want to change so much.

It makes me impatient.

I need to remember the lessons of the ducks:

don't rush, simply put one little webbed foot in
front of the other.

Dear God, when I feel that I am walking on ice,

when I slip on confrontations with loved ones,

help me remember

the ducks who walk on ice—

carefully.

Dear

God,

I

feel

lonely.

No one seems to understand why I care for animals.

"There are homeless and hungry people.

    You need to care for them," I am told.

So much is closed off.

I don't want arguments.

Why must caring be apportioned,

    First here, then there?

Is that how we experience You?

(They want me to care less.

But You allowed my heart to grow.

I cannot and will not shrink it back now.)

Now—when I have found Your Love

    in the furry and the scaled,

    In the feathered and the prickly spined?

Please help me—

    Give me words

    Give me wisdom

    Give me patience

Help me,

    as I pray for

        The hungry and the homeless

        The fur-wearer,

            scale-bearer,

                feathered and

                    prickly spined.

For parents of a child who has been teased for caring about animals

Dear God,
A caring child has been laughed at.
She has been mocked; she has been teased.
She is home, now, sad and upset.
Her friends do not understand.
They have grasped, though, that caring makes one
      vulnerable.
She is vulnerable, God.
Caring for Your vulnerable world makes her so.
Embrace her God as she embraces Your Creatures
    And embrace her friends, too,
      so that they may know
    A Love that asks to be shared,
      a caring that reaches toward others.

For Our Special Friendships with an Animal Who Lives with Us

God of cats and God of dogs

God of all those who live in our homes with us

God of dogs and God of cats

Of gerbils and guinea pigs

Of rabbits and rats

God of all beings who reside here, beneath this roof

Thank You for gathering us together.

Thank You for the love we share.

Keep our household safe.

Help us take care of each other.

God, thank You for this roof and the blessings of
friendship it shelters.

God of furry beings,
I remember the animals of my childhood.
The animals who knew my voice
    who welcomed my hands
    who accompanied me as I grew.
I remember my love for them
    and my sense of their love for me.
I remember them in the summer
    warmth and radiance.
I remember them in the winter
    security and presence.
I became the person I am now
    because as a child I loved animals.
    And I carry their memory deep within.
Deep within, I remember feeding them,
      caring for them
      worrying about illness
      and the shock of their deaths.
They taught me about caring and about mourning.
Through them, I learned to love deeply and to receive
      wordless love.
Through them, I learned about relationships and
      sharing.

Through them, I was a child of God in Your Creation:
 free, content, blessed.
Thank you for these blessings.
Thank you for this small miracle of Your Creation

When I was a child,

I loved an animal

And an animal loved me.

When an animal joins your household

Dear God,

Thank You for the presence of *(name)* in our lives.

We welcome *(name)* here to our home.

We promise to care for *(name)*

    To feed and protect *(name)*.

We will try to protect *(name)* from harm.

We promise to seek help for *(name)*

    if she/he becomes ill.

God, we are grateful for our new friend.

Bless our friendship.

Thank You for this life.

Thank You for this Love.

For the blessing of companion animals

God, thank you for *(name)*.
Watch over *(name)*.
Keep *(name)* safe.

Creator, bless *(name)*.
May *(name)* know love from his/her family.
May her/his family know her/his love.
May her/his family be faithful.
Friend, protect *(name)* and keep him/her from harm.
Help her/his family care for her/him.
Keep them all fed and sheltered.

Faithful One, please be with all animals who are
        suffering
All animals who have been abandoned
All animals who do not know love.
Holy Presence, increase our love.
Help us be faithful to *(name)*.
And help us care for all animals.

God, today I pray on behalf of my special friend.
I cherish each day we share together.

May all beings be happy.
May all beings know peace.

God, today, I pray on behalf of my special friend
Because he is ill.

May all beings be happy.
May all beings know peace.

I ask that Your healing spirit abide here,
May he know comfort and peace.

May all beings be happy.
May all beings know peace.

God, his illness scares me.
Release my anxiety.

May all beings be happy.
May all beings know peace.

Guide me as I make decisions.
Be present to us as we seek help.

May all beings be happy.
May all beings know peace.

God, thank You for Your presence in our lives.
I cherish each day we share together.

May all beings be happy.
May all beings know peace.

Dear God,

I think I know how much You love me.
I think I know how much You love me because
  (name) shows me.
Through Your animals, through *(name)*
  I know You listen to me.
Because of Your animals, because of *(name)*
  I know You care about me.
With Your animals, with *(name)*
  I am able to sense Your presence.
Thank You for the animals,
  thank You for *(name)*
  and thank You for Your love—
    which comes in different shapes and sizes.

My animal friend is getting old, Timeless One.

I know it. And it scares me.

She is sleeping more.

I don't know what to do.

Help me to learn how to take care of her, God.

Help me to learn to live with the changes she is going
through.

I pray for the hands of the vet.

May they be steady and quick.

May they be careful and sure.

May they repair and may they heal.

May they be Your hands.

Comforter, the dog who lives with a nearby family
        has disappeared.
The fliers in our neighborhood call to us, LOST DOG.
Holy One, I pray for the dog.
        May the dog be safe.
        May the dog stay safe.
        May the dog be reunited with her family.
Loving One, I pray for the family.
        May they be comforted in their sadness.
        May they be persistent in their search.
        May they be reunited with their friend.
Comforter, I pray for my neighborhood.
        May we be alert and supportive.
Faithful One, I pray for a happy reunion,
        And for the rejoicing that will be.

Prayers of Mourning and Grief

Dear God,

As an elephant's trunk hangs limply to the ground,

   So you find me here today, grief-stricken.

If like an elephant I could gather with others,

With branches and earth to bury my friend,

If we, together, could stand vigil all night long

   perhaps this loss, shouldered by many would be

      bearable.

I was not ready for my friend to die.

Hold me God.

Keep me God.

This death, once unthinkable, is now the only thing I

   think about.

Give me friends who understand.

Maybe then I could slide into the place I used to

   occupy.

The world is so heavy upon me.

Give me shoulders like the elephant to carry it.

Comfort me, O Presence.

Be with me, O Comforting One.

Comfort me, as I cry and lumber through the world.

I cannot comprehend that we have lost *(name)*.

I know that we didn't really lose *(name)*.

But it is hard to say *died*.

And if it is hard for me to say *(name)* died,

How will my child be able to say it?

How will my child be able to live with it?

Help me reach out to my family.

Give me words of comfort—

    God, You know that I need them.

Give me a gentle way,

    though God You know what rages and surges

      inside.

May Your Love embrace us, as we embraced *(name)*.

God, abide with us in our mourning.

Find us God.

Don't let go.

A mourner's prayer

My whole body feels sad
O God of light
O God of night
My muscles are tight
My eyes fill with tears
Sometimes my head hurts from this sadness.
My heart is sinking into itself with heaviness
      and my heart is tearing apart with grief.
God, please send Your healing breath upon me.
Breath into my muscles.
Wipe my tears.
Cradle my head.
Bring me into Your immense heart.
Help me with my sadness, God of healing.
O God of night
Tell me that someday I'll feel all right.

Dear God,

Help me let go.

God of creatures great and small,

Help me, the living, let go of the dead.

I cannot do it alone, O Compassionate One.

I need Your help.

Help me say good-bye to my friend.

Dear God,

Help me let go.

Help me, the living, let go of the dead.

Dear God,

Today, I want just to remember *(name)*.

    I remember the joy of her arrival

    I remember the way she walked.

    I remember the way she smelled.

    I remember our special moments.

    I remember morning greetings
       and evening rituals.

    And I remember how she died.

Dear God, it is good to remember—what a special
    friendship!

But God, it is hard to remember—because now she is
    gone.

Help me to be thankful for her life as I mourn her
    death.

When your child dreams about your animal friend
after he or she is dead

Dear God,

Please stay near us today.

Last night my child dreamed that *(name)* was alive.

It was a wonderful dream

    they played together

    and they talked together

    and they relaxed together—

    just as before.

Everything seemed all right in the dream.

But now my child is awake and knows it was just a

    dream.

My child is heartbroken,

    the dream has reawakened her grief.

I wish her dream were true.

She woke up and was so sad.

Help me God, help me with words to speak.

Help me tell her that even if forgetting seems easier,

    it is good to remember.

Help me explain that, maybe, You gave her this dream

    as a gift—

    the gift of memory.

The memory of a wonderful animal friend.

We still miss *(name)*

Thank You for *(name)*.

And thank You for this dream.

Dear God,

This morning Your whole of Creation greeted me,
    as it does each morning.
    Squirrels, as usual, were busy with a labyrinth of
        tree limbs
    ducks dipped and shook in rhythm in a
        synchronized swim.
Everywhere I looked I saw Your Creation.

But I stop, hit full force by the aching sense of loss.
Someone I loved deeply is dead.
I loved him so.
He had asked so much of me, so much care, so much
    nurturing.
He taught me about the deep places inside of me.

I think I am doing fine, he has been dead for so long
    now.
But the amnesia that covers my grief deprives me of
    the memory of him, too.
He was so alive, too—like all of us this morning.
When I encounter my grief, a hole opens up.
It swallows so much.
First to go are my words.

How hard it is to speak of this!

I feel again the breaking of my heart.

But perhaps to know that I feel it breaking tells me

    I have distanced myself from the immediate

      heart-stopping grief of his death.

Now I understand it is a wound,

    a wound that will not kill me,

      though at one time it felt as though it would.

Can I receive the life of today, the glorious morning

      life that greets me here?

    God, I miss him so.

    I take comfort from Your animals just in their

      living.

I will take comfort, but I know, as I am sure You

      know, that I will be back,

    back with my wounded heart

    and the knowledge that the wounding is perhaps

      a sad gift from You, too.

I am more whole now, knowing I loved, than I was

      before my heart was broken.

Dear Comforter,

I've been thinking about the story of a little girl
  named Jessie and a dead sparrow.

  Encountering the dead bird, Jessie insists on a
    funeral.

  At the burial she prays, DEAR GOD, BE KIND TO
    THE SPARROW, OR I'LL KILL YOU.

  The storyteller thinks this prayer reveals her
    fear—

  the sparrow's death perhaps reminding her of her
    own mortality.

But God, though I can't know what she meant,

  I wonder if she wasn't really angry with You.

  You let the sparrow die.

  How could You?

  And perhaps she also displays a healthy theology.

  If You aren't taking care of the sparrow—

  If, in a sense, You haven't let the sparrow into
    heaven,

  Well then God, I don't want anything to do with
    You.

  I'll kill You off—that is what I'll do.

  If You aren't powerful enough
    and compassionate enough

to care for a dead sparrow,
Well, You aren't powerful enough and
compassionate enough to be my God.
Our God.
God, she isn't the first or the last to feel that way.
After all, if You can't take care of the sparrows of
this world
when they are alive,
then at least console us with the knowledge they
are included in Your heaven.
But God, I don't want to kill You off.
I want You everywhere.
I want Your power and compassion encompassing all
animals.
O God, I shall try to do my part,
my God-given part of approaching animals with
compassion
and using whatever human power I possess to
encourage compassion.
God, I will try faithfully to do my part here on Earth.
I will leave Heaven to You.
Please God, don't let Jessie down.

I am not lettered in words about You, God.

    Theology.

    Well, let's say

    I'm left dancing on a pin

    trying to grasp some of its certainties.

But God, words don't completely fail me yet.

    Why shouldn't animals have souls?

Do we want to reserve only a part of heaven for
        them?

    A little door off to the side, maybe?

    As though it were even ours to decide?

When we mourn an animal, we ask the certainty of
        heaven for them.

That is because there is something we know that no
        amount of words can undo—

    We knew them as individuals.

    We knew a certain glance, a definite response.

    We knew wonderment.

    We experienced their soulfulness.

And though words may rain down on us that this is
        not so

    We know otherwise.

    I pray You do, too.

The soulfulness of animals greets me every day.

And from the nearness of that soulfulness I can sense
        it in far away
                places, too.
Right now.
                The seas and oceans and rivers must be
                    flowing with it
                the deserts and the forests and icy regions of
                    the world
                        are teeming with it
                and the barn nearby
                and the zoo
                and the circus.
    All animals, our God partners.
What would such soulfulness require of us?
    Not only words.
    But we begin somewhere, and here I am God,
Beginning again with You and Your animals,
    Name me as one of them.

God, this prayer startles me.

For Caring One, I want to thank You for the grief I
feel.

God, I am still grieving.

I am burdened by grief—

Jagged and sharp, it pierces me.

Yet, Loving One, is my grief a gift?

It teaches me what I care about.

I did not know I could care this deeply.

I did not know I could survive such grief

Jagged and sharp, and persistent.

But, God, that is why I thank You

For now I understand

Caring this deeply does not kill me.

Thank You God, for now I understand

Compassion includes grief

As much as prayer includes You.

For an animal whose human companion dies

Dear God,

Please be present to *(name)*,

    the friend of *(name)*.

Comforter, be with this friend.

What a loss!

More than anyone, she knew *(name)*.

    She knew mornings and evenings of

        companionship.

    She knew feedings and

        She knew friendship.

God, how you blessed their friendship!

But now that has all changed.

Let not the human community which also mourns

    forget her.

May she be safe with a new friend.

May she again know

    The joy of mornings and evenings together.

    May she be fed by someone who loves her.

    May she be given friendship again.

I ask this God, because I know that Love is of You

    and from You.

That Love can do all things.

Prayers of Petition and Intercession

May all creatures
    Those beginning to breathe
        And those ending their breath
    Those alone
        And those in herds
    Those ill
        And those healthy
May all creatures
    Know Your Love.

O Animals,

I pray for the humans who are in your lives.

If you live with a kind human, I am thankful.

If you live with a troubled human

> I pray they do not take their troubles out on you.

If you live where there is an abuser present

> I pray for intervention and protection.

If you live in a confinement facility

> Not knowing a day of slaughter soon will
> confront you.

> I pray for compassionate people to enter your
> life.

If you live in the nearby forest

> I pray that we leave it undeveloped.

If you live in the wild

> I pray for hunters to put down their guns.

If you live across the seas

> I pray that you are unmolested by the curious
> Uncaptured by the mercenary.

I pray for each of you who lives on land

> That you might have Earth beneath your feet
> That rushing cars or hunters or bulldozers will
> not destroy you.

I pray for each of you who lives in the seas

    That you might have clean water

    That nets or spears or hooks will not harm you

    That sonar noises will not injure you.

O Animals, I pray for your safety.

For a stray dog you saw

Dear God,
Today, I saw a dog running by the road.
No one was near the dog.
I did not stop.
I could not stop . . . .
I hesitate, God, because
        You know whether that is true.
I confess, God, I did not help.
    Forgive me.
But God,
I am worried about this dog.
Is she still safe?
So many cars were rushing by.
I am frightened that the dog might have been
        hit.
God, I passed by that dog.
Please, God, don't pass by.
Be here with me and
    Be with that dog.
        Keep us both safe.
And God,
    Help me
        Next time to stop.

Hear my Prayer, O God,
    for all lost and lonely and wounded animals
        in the world
            including me,
                I pray.
Hear my prayer.
    Be with all lost and lonely and wounded animals
        in the world,
            including me,
                I pray.

Sometimes we hear on the radio or television, or read on the Internet about an animal who is suffering or in trouble. This prayer is for those times.

Dear God,

I heard about an animal in trouble.

Yet, God, I am so far away from this animal.

I feel stricken by his suffering and saddened by my own powerlessness.

I cannot save this animal by reaching out my arms in rescue.

But I can do this.

I can pray for this animal's safety.

Please God, keep this animal safe.

Prayer for animals in shelters

May you know the touch of kindness.

May you know a warm blanket, a special treat.

May you know a walk outside.

May you know another day.

For homeless beings

God of warmth, Your world has turned very cold.
I pray for homeless animals.
>They once knew welcome but now only know
>>scavenging and danger.
>The cold is hard on them.
>The life on the street or the alley or the field is
>>difficult.
>Shelters for them may be dead ends.
>In the park, it is too cold for the insects,
>>and the birds who are wintering there will
>>>find few of them this day.

Your bitter wind blows fierce this winter.
I worry about homeless people, too.
>And pray not just for shelters to welcome them,
>But the skill of people to help them with their
>>next step.
So many issues—addiction, mental illness, violence—
>keep humans on the street, away from home.
God of the night, I pray for blankets and safety.
>I pray for warmth.

Blankets, safe shelter, food—

God is this the dividing line of each cold day and night

      for all homeless beings?

    I want to enclose all who feel Your bitter wind

    within my arms,

        saying, IT WILL BE ALL RIGHT.

    I want to help make these words true.

    Surely I am not alone.

God, Your wind also picks up leaves and swirls them

      through the air.

Pick up my words and swirl them together with

    the spirits of all who pray

      for those in the cold.

O God of great and small and the in-between.

I know of your presence in my life.

You have touched me.

Sometimes, I feel Your touch through the presence of
      other animals.

So much is revealed!

Your animals teach me about how amazing and
      bounteous life is.

God, we walk on this earth, with two legs or four, six,
      or eight or a hundred.

Thank You for all the animals.

God, right now, in the midst of thankfulness,

    I remember all the animals who are kept from
      walking.

Who are in cages or crates

    Who are bred to grow so big their legs
      can no longer support them.

    Those whose limbs are broken.

Be with them, O healing God.

    Be with us all.

I pray we humans may still learn to walk humbly with
    You, God,
      and Your creatures.

Dear Friend,

The dodo ran toward humans

In a forest being logged,

One last Ivory-Billed Woodpecker was spotted.

The Passenger Pigeon and Heath Hen fell to the
      growth of cities,

    Guns did not help.

The Great Auk, well, You know that story—

They had never known predators.

God, they had never been persecuted
    until they met human beings.

God, the list of extinct species grows.

What would You have us do?

I run toward You, Friend.

I trust that You hear me.

For the hubris of our ancestors that said, THIS IS MINE
    Forgive us.

Of our hubris, here and now, cure us.

Teach me how to be a friend
    to feathered and unfeathered

Teach me to remember THIS IS YOURS.

I pray there is still time.

Dear God,

A cow jumped over a slaughterhouse fence and
     escaped.

For her freedom, I am thankful.

For her continued safety, I pray.

Safety, O Loving Presence, is needed by so many.

I remember a time when I needed all cows inside that
     fence.

     They were captives to my desires.

God, there are fences I need to jump, too.

     You know what keeps me captive.

     You know what keeps my thoughts from You.

     You know what limits me.

     I stay comfortable with the old,

          with narrowed ambitions and selfish desires.

Help me leap over fences that keep me from You.

Thank you for leaps of faith and leaps of desperation.

May those unsafe and those who are too safe jump for
     freedom!

God, You are everywhere.

It is I who cannot always see You, cannot always
behold You.

You are in the morning sunrise and the clouds that
block it.

You are in my friendships and even in my enemies.

You are in what I treasure and what I take for granted.

It is hard for me, God, to imagine You in the
slaughterhouse.

Is it possible You are there?

I know You are everywhere:

You are in the revealed and the hidden,

The joyful and the painful.

You must be there in the killer and the killed.

Now I see, God.

You are needed there.

Those who kill need You.

And those who are killed need You.

Clouded or not, the sunrise will always reveal You.

Befriended or alienated, my friendships will always
contain You.

And God, until it ceases to exist,
the slaughterhouse will always need You.

In and through You, we gain our breath.

You, the God of babyhood and new beginnings,

the God of first steps and a steadying hand.

When we were most needy, You came to us through

the care of others.

Your presence filled our days as we began to meet the

world

with our next steps and our curious hands.

I rejoice in babyhood and the joy of new life.

I rejoice in the tenderness of age in response to the

neediness of the young.

I rejoice in breastfeeding and nourishing the young.

Every one a miracle.

O God, when I think of the love that each baby needs,

I think, too, of calves.

I am so saddened that calves are taken from their

mothers.

Why do we do this?

Why do we kill caregiving?

Why do we see ourselves as more important than

a calf and his mother?

God of justice, I am so saddened by injustice.

I grieve for the mother cow,

the baby calf,

their separation.

O Compassionate One, have compassion on me—
    a startled, and saddened child of God.
Begin again, with me.
    I need the tenderness given those during the early
        years of life,
            tenderness because my feelings are so raw.
    I need the nurturance given those during the
        growing years
            so that my spirit may grow, encompassing
            the unjust as well as the just—
                just as You do.
God, thank You for the gift of compassion.
And please, God, please be present to Your cattle until
    we humans are.

If I had a God's-eye view of the world,

I'd be scared, God.

I would see forests turned into pasture.

I would see animals losing their homes,

    Trampled and injured as the trees are destroyed.

There are three times as many animals being

    destroyed to become food

    As there are people on this Earth.

I cannot comprehend twenty billion animals destined

    to be eaten,

    Can You?

    For what?

I would not want to lose my home, God.

I would not want to be born to be eaten.

Sometimes I think we need to learn—

    What pity means

    What repentance means.

Turning away is so much easier than turning toward.

Turning away is so much easier than repairing.

Turning away means we do not have to change.

We humans are good at turning away.

Maybe a God's-eye view of the world is more painful

    even than this awareness—

    of habitat loss and unloving treatment of Your

    creatures.

Where are You God

You with Your God's-eye view of the world?

    The diminishing world?

    The damaged world?

        Are You scared too?

Dear God,

I saw a dead fox on the side of the street yesterday.

She was near a small wooded area.

I felt sorry for her death, and I marveled that she had
      survived here at all—

    Bordering one of our major overloaded
      highways,

        a small fox had maneuvered and survived.

But we had taken so much away from her before she
      was killed.

We are creating the world in our image, it seems,
    an image of concrete and palatial houses, and
    shopping centers.

How hard it is in our concrete world to remember
    the others who need space for their living.

Surely, there is something I can do to help protect
    the habitats of my sisters and brothers.

Dear God, I know the city is winning.

Our relentlessness is robbing others.

    Not only *ours*, which might mean someone else's,
    but *my* relentlessness . . . .

For it could have been my car that killed the fox.

I am no bystander.

I, too, am a part of this urban growth.

This encroachment.

But now I seek inner growth.

To enable me to see the fox's world,

     And to envision that I myself can let go

     of the relentlessness that mowed one fox down.

God of completeness,

    God of Compassion

        I pray for animals in laboratories—

The drugged

The burned

The addicted

The tortured animals.

These animals in laboratories . . . why are they there?

    Through no action of their own.

    No animal suffers from addiction, until we make
      them.

    Victim . . . it seems the most appropriate word.

    Victim of our inability to keep our hands off.

And God, where does this lead?

To anger first.

Then to protest.

We call You God of Compassion.

We pray for some of that compassion now.

    God remember the lambs.

    God abide with the rabbits.

    God be with the chimpanzees.

    God remember the rats.

God abide with the cats.

God be with the pigs.

God of completeness,

    God of Compassion

        I pray for animals in laboratories.

Dear God,

A world of cages and barren spaces

    Poking and prying

    Misuse and then dying

    Is all that some animals know of Your Creation.

They have been called *lab animals*.

Are they not innocent animals?

Great God, transform us,

    we who are not innocent.

We know of Your empowering ways. Be with

    protestors. Empower their actions.

We know of Your transforming ways. Be with

    experimenters. Transform them.

We know of Your revelatory ways. Be with leaders.

    Enlighten them.

God, we know of Your comforting ways.

    Be with animals in laboratories.

    Comfort them until the word *lab* no longer

    defines their world.

Free them, O God, from humans

    and free us, Creator, from words and actions that

    confine You or them.

Brother chimpanzee, sister capuchin

For this moment, I am holding you close,

I am holding you here.

Brother bonobo, sister mangabey,

I pray for you.

Brother macaque, sister gibbon,

I pray for your habitats

Brother mandrill, sister gorilla,

I pray for your families

Brother monkey, sister ape,

I pray for your health.

Brother baboon, sister orangutan,

It is hard to remember you always.

Brothers and sisters,

The human world steps between you and me.

But brothers and sisters,

For this moment, I am holding you close,

I am holding you here.

Yes, I am listening!

> Tell me, Coyote, of the loss of your home to
> bulldozers,
> Of how you have survived,
> And where you can hide from iron leg-traps.
>> You sing, O Coyote.
>> I am listening.

Dear God, help us listen and teach us to help.

Yes, I am listening!

> Tell me, Gibbon, of your life in the Cardamom
> Mountains,
> Of how you survived the Cambodian wars,
> And of how hunters follow your songs and kill
> you
>> You sing, O Gibbon.
>> I am listening!

Dear God, help us listen and teach us to help.

Yes, I am listening!

> Tell me, Turkey, of your stressful confinement,
> Of how you cry when your beak is sliced with a
> hot blade,

And of how You thrash and strain and flail
against death.
You sing, O Turkey.
I am listening.

Dear God, help us listen and teach us to help.

Creator and Sustainer:

Thank You for sanctuaries, where rescued animals
may live safely.

Please be with those who are at risk
because of the shocking way they have been bred.

Please be with the birds blinded by ammonia fumes or
cockfighting
and with pigs and turkeys lame because they have
lived longer than
humans "decided" they were meant to.

Help the injured survive their injuries.

Help their human companions who see how the
injuries and disabilities
Prevent Your animals from being as physically
whole as they might be.

O God, be with all the animals on sanctuaries.

For those who create such a safe space, I pray.

For their joys of knowing and caring for rescued
animals, I pray.

For the sadness and grief that walks hand in hand with
their joys,
Dear God, I pray.

We cannot protect the sanctuary workers from grief—
  Grief comes because they love well.
But surely we can help them to know their grieving is
    surrounded by
    invisible hands who wipe the tears,
    invisible arms who wrap them in a hug of
      support and understanding,
    an invisible presence that announces,
    YOU ARE NOT ALONE.
Dear Creator and Sustainer, I ask You to reside in each
    holy place that is a sanctuary
    and to help us as we try to restore the world as a
      holy place,
    a sanctuary, a safe space, for all Your Creation.

O Holy One,
Sometimes I wish my eyes had not been opened.
Yes, the suffering I learn about and see hurts me too
   deeply.
   But, O Forgiving One,
To know that I was the cause of that suffering!
How does one live with that knowledge of years upon
   years
   of use of Your Creation, of Your beings?
I have unknowingly been a part of a cruel, human
   world.
Yes, I renounce it!
Yes, I witness against it!
   But, O Comforting One,
Where does that leave me?
   O Healing One,
I am fractured by this knowledge, this pain.
I need forgiveness to wash over me and through me,
   to purge me.
I am estranged even from myself.
My selfishness assails me.
The lives lost haunt me.
I want to feel release from this overwhelming sense of
   responsibility.

No, not just responsibility—

Blame.

I want to believe if I had known earlier I would have changed earlier.

But even more, I seek forgiveness because I fear this is not so.

Merciful and Loving God,

I confess that I have erred and strayed from Your ways
like the human I am.

I confess that I think in terms of owning, possessing,
acquiring.

I confess that I have not learned how to share.

I confess that arrogantly, I act as though ruler of my
own kingdom.

I confess that I have cut myself off from everyone and
everything that makes my comfort possible.

I confess that this self-centeredness imperils the Earth
and all beings.

For thinking of myself as separate from Your
Creation, forgive me.

For my part in exploiting, using, abusing, dissecting,
wearing, eating, imprisoning,
experimenting on, displaying, hunting, fishing,
and enslaving
Your creatures,
forgive me.

For my part in exploiting, using, destroying, paving
over, polluting, poisoning
Your Creation,
forgive me.
Transform my self-deceptions, God.
Anchor me again in Your Creation.
Re-create me. Make me whole and wholly Yours.

O Healing One,

  To whom may I turn for forgiveness?

O Source of Connection,

  Teach me forgiveness.

O Forgiving One,

  Restore me.

O Restoring One,

  Abide with me in my struggles.

O Source of Hope,

  I am here.

Holy One, rescue me from useless anger and feelings
of futility.
Point my attention to animal sanctuaries for
grounding in real lives.
Loving One, rescue us from despair that we are not
doing more.
Remind us, each of us, we must begin somewhere.
And balance our grief at the loss of beloved animals
with gratitude for the opportunity to know them.
Help me create a safe space within,
where the lives of all those in sanctuaries may be
cherished.
With gratitude for safe spaces and safe-keeping,
I pray.
Hear my prayer and may those in sanctuaries know
that I pray for them.

Did Jonah in escaping You, seize the opportunity to
    learn about Your Sea Creatures?
Yes, I know, he was running away from You.
But did he not dive headlong into another life?
What might he have taught us about that Leviathan?
A prophecy of marine life?
We need that now, God.
Send us from Ninevah headlong into the Sea, God.
A sea full of blood.
Deliver us, God, from destroying your Sea Creatures.
    Help us repent.
Swallow us, God.
Make us new.

May we be Your people unfolding a new possibility

May we be Your hands to the suffering

May we be Your feet in protest

May we be Your shouts in anger

May we be Your tears in mourning

May we touch Your animals and change the world.

May we be Your people unfolding a new possibility.

God, please do—

    in relationship with us—

Better than we have done

    in relationship with them.

Evening Prayers

God, today I had all the time in the world.

I went for a walk.

The sidewalk showed signs that slugs had crossed over
them.

Birds were calling to each other in the trees.

I felt Your breath through the breeze.

God, You were living and breathing through Your
Earth, weren't You?

And all seemed just right.

Just right, walking through Your Creation.

Fill the blanks with references to what you have done
on behalf of animals

Today, God, I prayed with my mouth.
 I spoke out on behalf of animals.
Today, God, I prayed with my hands.
 I _ _ _ _ _ _ _ _ _ _ _ _ _ _ _.
Today, God, I prayed with my body.
 I _ _ _ _ _ _ _ _ _ _ _ _ _ _ _.
God, my prayer says I will remember you.
I will remember You, God, all my days and nights.
And I will remember Your creatures, O Creator, all
 my nights and days.

Dear God,

Here we go again. Another day. Another day.

And here I am again. I am so weary.

It is so hard to see the world this way—

    thinking about and loving animals.

That is why I am here again, even though I am so

    tired.

I am here again. Here again, in Your presence.

Yes God, you have given me awareness.

Yes God, you have given me love.

But, I need something more, O Generous One.

I pray to be restored.

O God, be here again.

Early this morning, I saw a child and a dog.

God, they were happy!—tail wagging, child skipping,
    they headed off for an adventure.

Was it summer,
        and they explored the neighborhood?

Was it fall,
        and they swished their way through the leaves?

Was it winter, and their snowprints—
    dog's paws, child's boots,
    dog's paws, child's boots—
        told the story of their walk?

Or was it spring
    With muddy tracks and new shoots
    And the sense of new beginnings and fresh
      growth?

God, I know that path they walked.

Those are my footprints, too.

I have known so many new beginnings since I made
        those tracks and walked with that dog,
    loved that dog.

New beginnings, yet old losses that still feel
      fresh.

God, thank You for vivid memories.

Thank You for that dog's life—well-lived, well-loved.
God, thank You because
early this morning, I saw a child and a dog.

Dear God,

What have I achieved today?

God, after all this time, only fragments.

It makes me feel broken,

I don't want to be broken, not again and again.

This brokenness, God, it is painful.

Help me find You in my brokenness.

Help me let go into Your arms, Your wings, Your fins.

Is that what happened today, God?

Did You embrace my brokenness?

You hear of my loneliness

   and I am no longer alone.

You hear of my brokenness

   and I am no longer broken.

My brokenness is yet another way to find You,

    Friend.

O God of mystery,

What a mysterious gift is life!

So much of my living is done without my awareness—

    I breathe without thinking

    My heart beats without thinking

    Such living does not require my thoughts,

        does not ask me to think about it.

But when I encounter my breathing, my heartbeat,

When I am aware of breathing in and breathing out,

This awareness leads me to Your mystery.

The breathing, the heart beating—

    these rhythms of life that require neither will nor
        control

    these rhythms of life that sustain me, sleeping and
        waking,

    what I am free to ignore

This is what links me to Your entire Creation.

This is what links me to all of the animals in Your
        Creation.

Together, we follow the rhythms of life.

Can I see You in them?

This evening, God, sharpen my awareness.

    Thank You for this animal body.

As I sleep, watch over me, God.

Watch over Your creation as with each new breath

    We come closer to a new day.

God, You are with me every moment.
Every moment, I am in the presence of the sacred.
Yesterday,
    I sat with someone nearby.
    The tail wreathing itself around,
    Majesty.
    I knew the presence of the sacred.
Today,
    Two blue jays working nearby
    Making a nest just outside my window,
    Creation.
    I am in the presence of the sacred.
Tomorrow,
    Will memory be enough?
    When I awake, can awe awaken too?
    The sacred hovers like a sea gull.
        It soars.
        It barks.
        It settles in my lap, contented.
God, You are with me every moment.
    Thank You.

Acknowledgments

Many animal advocates and animal lovers have shared with me their spiritual and emotional concerns. I am thankful for their work and for their openness. I am grateful for my friend, the artist Pamela Nelson, who created the Animal Prayer Rug for the cover of this book. As I worked on the prayers over the past several years, her supportive and inspiring presence in my life acted as an invitation to bring the prayers into existence. Pat Davis listened to and responded to several of the mourning prayers. I am grateful to Jane and Nancy Adams, Marie Fortune, and Pat Davis, who comforted me in my grief when rabbits we were caring for were killed. My editor, Evander Lomke, believed in this project and with his help, it became a better one. Through his own corporate prayers, my partner Bruce has taught me so much about how to pray.

Notes

p. 9. Evelyn Underhill, *Concerning the Inner Life* (Oxford: Oneworld, 2000), p. 47.

p. 29. In *The Variety of Life* (Oxford: Oxford University Press), Colin Tudge reports that "about a fifth of all known animals are beetles," (p. 287). It was British biologist J. B. S. Haldane who remarked that God seems "inordinately fond of beetles" (quoted by Tudge, p. 7).

p. 33. My *American Heritage Dictionary of the English Language* (4th Edition, 2001), does not contain entries for some of the animals I list in this prayer. The *Macmillan Illustrated Animal Encyclopedia* (1984, Philip Whitfield, ed.) provides these descriptions:
- *Angwantibo*, also known as the golden potto, is a West African primate.
- *Cavies,* a South American noctural rodent.
- *Moonrat*, a member of the hedgehog family, found in Cambodia. The survival of the Mindanao Moonrat, found in the Philippines and Mindanao, is threatened because of logging and slash-and-burn agriculture.
- *Tuco-tuco*, a South American rodent, who resembles North American pocket gophers.

p. 38. Enid Nemy, "Metropolitan Diary," *The New York Times*, December 17, 2000. Diary entry sent by Jacob Gasnick.